Just a Moment

Just a Moment

by

CECIL KERR

CHRISTIAN   JOURNALS   LIMITED
BELFAST :: DUBLIN :: OTTAWA

First Edition 1982 by Christian Journals Limited, BELFAST and
760 Somerset Street W, Ottawa, Ont. Canada.

Copyright © Christian Journals Limited 1982

ISBN 0 904302 77 6

Phototypeset by Mayne, Boyd & Son, Ltd., Belfast

Cover designed by Sandy Ferguson

Made in Ireland

Contents

More Than Conquerors

Peace of Christ

Hope Beyond Despair

Acknowledgements

Preface

Two years ago my good friend Richard Hodgett of the Newry Reporter asked me to write a weekly article for his paper. The response was a series called "Just a Moment" which has now appeared in three other provincial papers in Northern Ireland.

I want to express my sincere thanks to the editors of all four papers for their constant courtesy and encouragement: Andrew Doloughan, Banbridge Chronicle; Uel Troy, Coleraine Chronicle; Mervyn Dane, Impartial Reporter and Hal O'Brien, Newry Reporter.

It has been a real encouragement to me to receive messages of appreciation from all over the Province and abroad. I know there are many who will welcome this material appearing in a more permanent form. I am grateful to the Rev. Wilbert Forker of Christian Journals for so readily agreeing to publish this selection.

My prayer is that these reflections will lead every reader closer to Jesus who loves each one of us with an everlasting love.

My special thanks to Myrtle, my wife and my colleagues in the Christian Renewal Centre for their prayerful support and particularly to Lavinia Bowerman who so carefully typed these articles and presented them for publication.

I dedicate this book to all those who have helped me along the Christian way, some of whom are now in the nearer presence of the Lord they loved and served here on earth.

Cecil Kerr.
All Saints Day, 1981.

People I've Met

THE "PROF"

I am sure that one of the greatest influences in my early Christian life was the late Professor David Torrens. He was Professor of Physiology in Trinity College, Dublin and for many years Dean of the Faculty of Medicine in Dublin University. Born near Kilrea in Co. Derry he spent all of his working life in Dublin where he became almost a legend among succeeding generations of students, not only in the medical school but in many other departments as well.

It was my great privilege to meet the "Prof" as everyone called him shortly after I entered Trinity College. There were so many facets of his life and work that intrigued me. Most of all I saw in him the face of Christ. He never wrote a book and I never heard him preach a sermon but he lived the life of a devoted servant of Christ and countless men and women all over the world to-day have cause to praise on every remembrance of him.

A Life of Service

The "Prof" was not only an acknowledged expert in his chosen field of medicine but he was a world authority on clocks. He could have lived a life of relative ease and indulged in his own hobbies and interests. Instead his life was one of humble, self-effacing service to students from all walks of life and backgrounds. His simple rooms in the college became a haven for many who were lost and lonely and far away from home. The door was always open and constant cups of tea were brewed.

At any hour of the night he was willing to go out and see a student who was ill and many who found the emotional strain of university life too much for them had in him a ready listener and a good counsellor. As I came to know the "Prof" better I discovered the secret of his life. He had a deep personal faith in Christ which was kept alive by daily prayer and Bible Study. Hours before others awoke in the College the "Prof" was up to study his Bible and begin the day with prayer. He had a profound knowledge of the Scriptures. The Bible was for him a living Word which gave direction to his life and fuelled his selfless service. He never 'pushed Christianity down our throats' but the reality of his faith shone through his actions and opened up the way to conversations that changed many lives.

Wide Horizons

He loved the mountains of Switzerland and the Wicklow hills. Their majesty spoke to him of the God of creation whom He loved with childlike simplicity and their grandeur matched the vision in his heart. To those of us who had been bound in the prison houses of history and fettered by so many prejudices "Prof's" faith opened wide horizons of God's love for all men whatever their race or background.

When I think of the "Prof" now there is always a memory that inspires me to a new step of faith and I recall the words of Beatrice Cleland:

"Not merely by the words you say,
Not only in your deeds confessed
But in the most unconscious way
Is Christ expressed.

Is it a beatific smile?
A holy light upon your brow?
Oh, no – I felt His presence while
You laughed just now.

For me 'twas not the truth you taught,
To you so clear, to me still dim,
But when you came to me you brought
A sense of Him.

And from your eyes He beckons me
And from your heart His love is shed,
Till I lose sight of you, and see
The Christ instead.

Think on These Things:

"Blessed is the man
who walks not in the counsel of the wicked,
nor stands in the way of sinners,
nor sits in the seat of scoffers;
but his delight is in the law of the Lord,
and on his law he meditates day and night.
He is like a tree
Planted by streams of water,
That yields its fruit in its season,
And its leaf does not wither.
In all that he does, he prospers."　　　Psalm 1 vs. 1-3.

11

"MAN FROM THE MOON"

It's not every day you meet a man from the moon! Some time ago I had the great privilege of spending a week-end in the company of Colonel Charles Duke from Texas, U.S.A. Col. Duke has spent a record three days on the surface of the moon. In 1972 he took part in the 5th manned lunar mission which was the first scientific expedition to inspect, survey and sample materials and surface features in the Descartes region of the rugged lunar highlands.

It was fascinating to hear a first hand account of an experience which very few men have had the opportunity to share. Col. Duke tried to find words adequate to describe the grandeur of God's creation as it unfolded before his eyes from that rare vantage point out in space. It was all quite breathtaking to enter with him into those historic moments; to feel the lonely quietness of the moon's black surface; to share the excitement and thrill of new discoveries and to enter into some of the tension of those precarious hours when there was such a thin line between life and death and eternity was very near.

I shall never forget the way in which Col. Duke described the view that he had of our planet earth as he circled the moon. "It was set", he said, "like a beautiful jewel of blue and white on the black cushions of the darkness of space. And from that distance if you held up your hand you could block the earth from sight". I thought of those words which the Psalmist wrote several thousand years ago in Psalm 8:

"When I look at thy heavens, the work of thy fingers, the moon and the stars which thou hast established; what is man that thou art mindful of him, and the son of man that thou dost care for him? Yet thou hast made him little less than God, and dost crown him with glory and honour."

Psalm 8 vs. 3-5

A Search for God

What fascinated me more about Col. Duke was the story he told us of his search for God and his personal encounter with Jesus Christ as Saviour and Lord. He told us that when he was blasted off from earth into outer space he did not even pray and when he looked out on the wonders of creation he did not know the God who made it all.

It was several years after his moon mission that he made what he called "the greatest discovery" of his life. Though he had fame and the promise of fortune there was a deep emptiness in his life. He tried to fill that emptiness with work and pleasure and was finding himself increasingly addicted to alcohol. In such a state of emptiness and disillusionment his wife invited him to a Bible study week-end. It was there that the greatest miracle of his life happened *"the scales fell from my eyes as the Lord Jesus touched me and he completely changed my life."*

One Way to Unity on Planet Earth

Astronauts are noted for their toughness and self reliance but rarely have I seen someone who so reflects the love and tranquility that Christ gives. With tears in his eyes and love in his heart he spoke to an Irish audience drawn from all backgrounds and walks of life: *"He changed me completely"*, he said, *"and He can do that for you too. I am convinced there is only one way that we can come to unity on planet earth. Through Jesus alone can we be brought to one."*

You may reach for the moon and find it but if you have not had that personal meeting with Jesus Christ then you have missed life's greatest discovery.

Think on These Things:

"For what will it profit a man, if he gains the whole world and forfeits his life? Or what shall a man give in return for his life?"

Matthew 16 v. 26

Twice in recent years it has been my privilege to meet Mother Teresa of Calcutta. To meet her even briefly is an inspiration. She is a tiny, frail little person; as we say in Ireland, "you could almost blow her off your hand." Yet her presence commands a respect and a reverence. She has time for everyone. Her tired but piercing eyes are always open to detect "Christ in the distressing disguise of the poor" whether they are the helpless poor of the streets of Calcutta or the rich poor of the West, lost in selfish materialism. Her face shines with the love of Christ on whom her whole life is centred and there is a remarkable vitality in that frail body.

Let All be for Him Alone

Malcolm Muggeridge summed up her life in the pithy phrase which forms the title of the book which he wrote about her work: "SOMETHING BEAUTIFUL FOR GOD". Characteristically she would not allow him to write a biography. *"Christ's life"*, she said, *"was not written during His lifetime, yet He did the greatest work on earth – He redeemed the world and taught mankind to come to His Father. The work is His Work and to remain so, all of us are but His instruments, who do our little bit and pass by."*

Understandably Muggeridge was intrigued by her devoted life and work. Fortunately he was helped to see beyond the frail figure of Mother Teresa to the Lord who alone is the source and inspiration of her life. She wrote to Muggeridge: *"I think now more than ever you should use the beautiful gift God has given you for His greater glory. All that you have and all that you are and all that you can be and do – let all be for Him and Him alone."*

Thank God that all around the world there are tens of thousands of whom Mother Teresa is but our example. Where the Spirit of God can find a life that is yielded to Christ and willing to be a channel of His grace He can change the world.

A Living, Loving God

The story is told that when Jesus returned to Heaven after His resurrection an angel asked Him: "What plans have you made to carry on the work you began on earth?" He answered: "I have eleven men". "And what if they fail you?" said the angel. "I have no other plans". He replied.

"We need to find God", wrote Mother Teresa *"and He cannot be found in noise and restlessness. God is the friend of silence. See how nature – trees, flowers, grass – grow in silence; see the stars, the moon and the sun, how they move in silence. Is not our mission to give God to the poor in the slums? Not a dead God, but a living, loving God. The more we receive in silent prayer, the more we can give in our active life. We need silence to be able to touch souls. The essential thing is not what we say, but what God says to us and through us. All our words will be useless unless they come from within – words which do not give the light of Christ increase the darkness."*

Think on These Things:

"For by grace you have been saved through faith; and this is not your own doing, it is the gift of God – not because of works, lest any man should boast. For we are his workmanship, created in Christ Jesus for good works, which God prepared beforehand, that we should walk in them."

Ephesians 2 vs. 8-10

Billy Graham must be one of the best known Christian leaders in the world to-day.

Humility

On the occasions that I have met Billy Graham I have been impressed with his humility, faithfulness and compassion – all essential qualities of a true evangelist. I remember some years ago in Amsterdam when Christian leaders from all over Europe gathered for a Congress on Evangelism he took the trouble in the midst of a very busy programme to greet each delegate personally.

Faithfulness

On his last visit to Ireland Billy Graham came to address a meeting for students at Queen's University where I was then a chaplain. He gave a very moving address to a packed audience and he told me after the meeting was over that just as I introduced him he knew that God was urging him to switch from the message he had prepared. In a few moments he was on his feet giving an address that challenged every one of us to the core of his being. His address was "on preparing to die". I still remember the story he told about the heart-broken father who held his teenage daughter in his arms on the roadside when she was seriously injured in a car accident. "Dad", she said, "You taught me how to live a high life, you taught me how to drink, you taught me about being a social success but you never taught me how to die. Please tell me how to die." People listen to Billy Graham because he remains faithful to the basic truths of the Gospel of Christ whether he is addressing an audience of clever students or simple uneducated people in some backward part of the world. He knows that men's hearts need changing no matter what may be in their heads but he is sure that only the power of Christ can change the human heart.

Openess in Love

While remaining faithful to the fundamental truth of the Gospel, Billy Graham has a heart of love that will accept all those who put their faith and trust in Jesus Christ as Saviour and

Lord no matter what their race or background. In his worldwide
ministry of evangelism he has seen that:

"In Christ there is no East or West
In Him no South or North
But one great fellowship of love
Throughout the whole wide earth."

I have often heard him say that so much of his work in mass
evangelism would be unnecessary if all the churches were alert
to their responsibility for evangelism and every believer was a
living witness to Christ. The passion that fires this man of God is
well summed up in the words of Henry Tweedy:

"Blow, wind of God!
With wisdom blow
From mists of error, clouds of doubt,
Which blind our eyes to thee!
Burn, winged fire!
Inspire our lips
With flaming love and zeal,
To preach to all thy great good news,
God's glorious commonweal!"

Think on These Things:

*"For I am not ashamed of the gospel: it is the power of God for
salvation to every one who has faith."*

Romans 1 v. 16

17

"FROM DEATH TO LIFE"

I met a remarkable man on Easter Sunday. The Rev. Francis Paul is a minister in the Anglican Church of the Sudan in North Africa. He is a living proof of the resurrection, for like his Lord and Master he was wrongfully condemned to die. A miracle saved his life.

The Crucible of Suffering

During the civil war which raged in the Sudan for seventeen years Christians were badly persecuted and many met a martyr's death. Tens of thousands fled the country and thousands of others went into hiding in the bush where many starved to death. Yet in the midst of such deprivation and suffering the Church of Christ grew strong. Suffering, as so often happened in history brought out the best in the Christian Community.

Why? Why? Why Me?

There was a day in his life that Francis will never forget. He was caught by the security forces accused of being a terrorist and condemned to die. His hands were tied and he was hung suspended upside down from a tree. Two of his companions were brutally killed beside him. Francis said: "I cried out to God but my prayer was a selfish prayer. I was saying to God – Why? Why? Why should I die at my age? What will happen to my wife and children?

Then he said: "God gave me the grace to pray a different prayer". I said: "Lord, I am still young. I want to tell others about your love. I don't want to die yet, but Jesus, if you want to see me to-day then I am ready". After that Francis was able to pray for the soldiers who had captured him and speak to them about Christ and His love for them.

Suddenly the attitude of the army commander changed. He ordered his men to cut Francis down from the tree, to await further information about him. The miracle happened; his innocence was proved; he was taken right from the gate of death and here he was with us in Rostrevor to share this wonderful news.

The Path Through Suffering

Joy is written all over Francis' face. His one desire is to tell men and women the Good News of the love of Jesus and His power to sustain us even in the face of tragedy.

Rarely have I met a man who has so personally lived through the experience which the Psalmist records in the best known of all the Psalms:

"EVEN THOUGH I WALK THROUGH THE VALLEY OF THE SHADOW OF DEATH, I FEAR NO EVIL; FOR THOU ART WITH ME;"

Think on These Things:

"And if children, then heirs, heirs of God and fellow heirs with Christ, provided we suffer with him in order that we may also be glorified with him."

Romans 8 v. 17

When God called us to establish the Christian Renewal Centre in 1974, Fanny Robertson was one of the founder members of the Community here. She was well-known all over Ireland and as Secretary of the Overseas Board of the Presbyterian Church she was known and loved in India and Africa. Our commitment in the Christian Renewal Centre to work and pray for spiritual renewal and reconciliation stirred within Fanny a vision which God had given her many years before. She had longed to see Protestants and Roman Catholics coming together to read and study God's Word and find His way of peace. In some remarkable ways God allowed her to participate in that vision. On a short visit to Malawi in Central Africa several years ago I met a Roman Catholic priest who expressed his thanks for the blessing that God had given him through Fanny's ministry during a conference for missionaries which she had helped to lead.

Victory Over the Fear of Death

A few months after Fanny joined us at the Christian Renewal Centre she discovered that she had cancer. It was naturally a great blow to her and to us all. In God's healing touch and through skilled medical care she experienced two years of remission from her illness. During that time God used her in some remarkable ways to be a blessing to many people who came here.

Through many trials and tribulations Fanny learned the truth of Christ's promise that He would never leave her nor forsake her. She came to terms with death and entered into Christ's victory over it. Some months before she died she gave a very moving testimony in the presence of people gathered from all over Ireland. She said:

"If, in the next few weeks or months you hear that I have died do not grieve or be distressed. Rejoice for I shall go to be with the Lord."

One day shortly before she died I was praying with Fanny in her room with a beautiful view facing west across Carlingford Lough. I shared with her two verses of the well-known hymn by John Newton – "Amazing Grace". I had only discovered those two verses now seldom sung but part of the original song. I know they were a blessing to her soul and they expressed her feeling even in her great weakness.

"Yes, when this flesh and heart shall fail
And mortal life shall cease
I shall possess, within the veil
A life of joy and peace.

The earth shall soon dissolve like snow;
The sun forbear to shine;
But God, who called me here below
Will be forever mine."

Fanny even chose the theme for her funeral service:

"Thine be the glory, risen conquering Son,
Endless is the victory thou o'er death hast won;"

A Faith for Life and Death

In the middle of a little notebook she had written 'TRIUMPH – ROMANS 8' in capital letters. The faith that sustained her in her final illness was the faith she had known all through her life. As a young girl she had come to know Jesus Christ as her personal Saviour and she had yielded her life to His service.

Fanny loved the Bible and knew it well. In the many Bibles which she left there is eloquent witness to her daily walk with God down the years. She had written in the fly leaves many words which had inspired her and which God had used to challenge her. These words copied into her Bible years before her death illustrate the call of God to which Fanny had responded:

"What does it matter if my plans are thwarted
My hopes denied, my longing unfulfilled
If thus His highest purpose be accomplished
The perfect pattern that His Love has willed
Yes what will matter on that glorious morning
When I behold my Saviour face to face
Save to have been "my utmost for his HIGHEST"
A human channel for His saving grace
Cost what it may of sorrow and distress
Of empty hands, of utter loneliness
I dare, not, Lord, be satisfied with less."

21

One morning in early Spring as I came through the gate of the Christian Renewal Centre something remarkable caught my eye. During the winter months workmen had laid tarmacadam on the footpath. Through that black, unyielding surface a beautiful little crocus had burst with a lovely smile to greet the early spring sunshine. There was a profusion of crocuses all over the lawn but this one had a special fragrance because it had conquered its hard unfriendly surroundings with cheerful simplicity.

The Silent Saints

I thought of many people whom I have met during my ministry who are just like that crocus. They have had to endure untold suffering and sometimes great pain but their clear and simple faith in Christ has shone brightly in the midst of it all. My mind went back to one dear old lady whom I met early in my ministry. She had had a hard life bringing up a large family in times when there was very little to go around. She lived in a tiny kitchen house which had the bare minimum of furniture. And yet it was a benediction to visit her. As we talked and prayed together I always sensed the deep peace of the presence of Christ in that simple house, and I never left without a sense of blessing.

Peace in the Midst of Conflict

The peace that surrounded that little old saint was the inward peace of Christ which passes human understanding; it was peace in the midst of the storm. All her children had gone away except the 'black sheep of the family'. He was an alcoholic and his marriage had broken up. He made life a misery for his dear old mother. He came home at all hours of the night and yet she would open the door to him and take him in despite all the abuse he showered on her. She never gave up hope that God would touch and change his life.

I had the privilege of ministering to my dear old friend a few hours before she died. It was then that I discovered the secret of her serenity. Over the bed in her simple bedroom was a little verse. It expressed the faith that had given her strength to face so much suffering and sorrow.

"God hath not promised
Skies always blue,
Flower-strewn pathways
All our lives through;
God hath not promised
Sun without rain,
Joy without sorrow,
Peace without pain.

But God hath promised
Strength for the day,
Rest for the labor,
Light for the way,
Grace for trials,
Help from above,
Unfailing sympathy,
Undying love."

Through the pain she knew the glory. When the moment of death came she just slipped away beyond the sunset where no clouds can gather, no storms will threaten and no fears annoy.

A Prayer

"Support us, O Lord, all the day long of this earthly life
Till the shadows lengthen and the evening comes;
The busy world is hushed, the fever of life is over and work is
done.
Then Lord, in your mercy grant us a safe lodging, a holy rest and
your peace at the last."

THE MOST IMPORTANT MEETING IN
MY LIFE

I am so glad that I had a personal encounter with Jesus while I was still in my teens, for that meeting has directed the whole course of my life. I am so glad that long before I ever knew Him He had expressed His love for me. For me the great wonder of being a Christian – Christ's one – is not that I have chosen Him but that He has chosen me.

God's Amazing Grace

The whole Bible conveys this amazing truth of God's grace. Perhaps nowhere is it more beautifully expressed than by St Paul in Ephesians 1 verses 4 and 5:

> *"Even as he chose us in him before the foundation of the world, that we should be holy and blameless before him. He destined us in love to be his sons through Jesus Christ, according to the purpose of his will."*

Although I had been brought up in a Christian environment it was first at the age of fourteen that I realized I had to make a personal response to that love that Jesus has for me. I thank God for those who told me of my need to respond and helped me in it.

Since that day I have met tens of thousands of people all over the world who have come into that personal relationship with God in Christ that we call 'a new birth'. For many it has been so vivid and dramatic that it has been like walking out of prison into freedom; from darkness into light. For others it has been like a flower opening almost imperceptibly to the warmth of the morning sunshine. For all it has been the beginning of a new life. The mystery of the new birth is so powerfully conveyed by St John in chapter 3 of his Gospel where he records our Lord's conversation with Nicodemus. Nicodemus was puzzled about the new birth and he asked: *"How can a man be born when he is old?"* Our blessed Lord replied:

> *"The wind blows where it wills, and you hear the sound of it, but you do not know whence it comes or whither it goes; so it is with everyone who is born of the Spirit".*

Sons of God

As I reflect on those years since I first became consciously and personally aware of Jesus Christ as my Saviour and Lord I remember so many of the ways that meeting has changed my life. I think of the specific ways that God has guided me. I think of His great mercy and love; of His constant forgiveness and His endless patience. Above all I thank God that He has made me His son through Jesus and brought me into the greatest family on earth and in heaven.

I am so glad that I can share that wonderful affirmation which St John makes in his epistle:

"Beloved, we are God's children now; it does not yet appear what we shall be, but we know that when he appears we shall be like him, for we shall see him as he is."

As I write this my deep desire and sincere prayer is that you might also make that great discovery – that Jesus Christ loves you personally. When he died on the cross He had you in His heart. His greatest longing and desire is that you should know Him and find the fullest purpose for which He created you.

Think on These Things:

"Come now, let us reason together, says the Lord: though your sins are like scarlet, they shall be as white as snow; though they are red like crimson, they shall become like wool."

Isaiah 1 v. 18

In Christ –
A New Creation

THE MIRACLE OF A NEW LIFE

Every Monday evening people from all backgrounds come together at the Christian Renewal Centre for a meeting of prayer, praise and scripture sharing. When the meeting was over one evening someone introduced me to Michael. I reached out my hand to greet him but quickly realized that he had no hand to take mine. Instead of hands he had steel grippers on both arms. He told me his story. It's a mighty miracle of God's power to change a human being.

A Terrible Hate

Some years before when he was in his late teens, like so many others in this land, his heart was filled with bitterness and hatred. He and some of his friends decided to make a bomb. In his own words – "to hit these evil oppressors and strike a blow for Irish freedom. However, it was no one but ourselves whom we almost ushered into a Christless eternity. Our bomb exploded all right, but as we were making it. One second I was holding the bomb, the next it blew up in my hands sending me hurtling through the air."

Saved from Death

Michael was rushed to hospital and saved from death with little time to spare. During four months in hospital he had loving care and good treatment and time to think. "I thought about God and religion and politics. I quickly realized what a mug I was to risk my life for politics."

He came out of hospital an atheist, disillusioned and with much bitterness still in his heart. He decided to return to study as he would no longer be able to do manual work. In the Technical College which he attended he met some people who talked to him of a God whom they knew personally and who loved them. This was all new to Michael and he listened with interest for he saw that they had something real in their lives.

A New Creature

After a long inner struggle one day the miracle happened in Michael's life. One Sunday afternoon he was sitting in the kitchen of his home when quite distinctly the words of the Lord in REVELATION chapter 3 verse 20 came into his mind:

"Behold, I stand at the door and knock; if anyone hears my voice and opens the door I will come in."

"I raised my head to gaze skywards through the window near the table at which I was sitting, and I said, 'Lord Jesus, I know that you died for me, please come into my life and make me as you want me to be.' He knocked – I opened the door – He came in. With my heart bursting for joy He came in. All my questions melted away as the Answer walked in. Christ Jesus became the centre of my life."

When Michael walked outside that afternoon he felt what countless others have experienced:

"Heaven above is brighter blue,
Earth around is sweeter green;
Something lives in every hue
Christless eyes have never seen;
Birds with gladder songs o'erflow,
Flowers with deeper beauties shine
Since I know, as now I know,
I am His and He is mine."

A lot has happened to Michael since then. I saw him recently when he returned to Ireland after obtaining a degree in law at an English University. He wants to devote the rest of his life to helping others experience the miracle of God's power to change their lives.

Think on These Things:

"Therefore, if any one is in Christ, he is a new creation; the old has passed away, behold, the new has come."

2 Corinthians 5 v. 17

29

"Surprised by Joy" is how C. S. Lewis described his pilgrimage from unbelief to a personal faith in Jesus Christ. It constantly amazes me to learn the varied ways by which God's Holy Spirit brings people to that step of faith that leads to certain knowledge and deep assurance. How do we meet the risen Christ in the world to-day? How does He reveal Himself to us?

I believe He comes to those who seek for Him and who want the new life He has promised to bring. There is a graciousness and gentleness about His coming. He does not force His way into our lives but He comes to us at our point of need.

Beyond the Shadows

Yours may be the experience of a Thomas whose faith in the risen Christ emerged from the crucible of doubt. Or it may be the experience of a Peter who responded to the challenge of the risen Lord to do a special work for Him. Or it may be the experience of a Mary Magdalene who in her moment of despair recognised her risen Lord. Her experience was well captured in a painting of that scene by Rembrandt:

It is very early in the morning and the sun is not yet risen; there is Mary in the shadows, by the tomb, thinking they had taken away Her Lord and not knowing where they had laid Him; but in the East the dawn is very faintly rising in the sky, and the risen Master is coming over the grass towards her – although she is still in the shadow, the faint light of morning is on His face. What will she do? Will she remain in the shadows or will she look up? This seems to me to be the situation which we are in today.

By birth, by nature we belong to the world of the shadow, but it is not necessary to remain there.

We can step out and recognise the risen Lord.

He Invited Me to Share My Hopes and Fears

A young medical student put his experience in words that speak for many in our day:

"It was hard for me
to realize that all my questions, all my doubts
on who I was, and why I was, and what I ought to be,
could not be answered.

and they remained
to haunt me in the silent times of loneliness,
when I had time to think, and ask . . . and find no answer.
'Why bother asking, then?' I thought.
'There is no answer anywhere'.
And then one day
I met a man:
a man who came beside me.
and showed me who I was, and why I was, and what I ought to be,
and who, with outstretched hand,
invited me to share my hopes and fears with him.
A dream? Delusion? Figment of my own imagination?
NO!
That hand was real, alive . . . and scarred."

When by faith we recognise the risen Lord we find ground for new hope for ourselves and for the world. We accept His challenge to service in the pattern of His costly love for mankind. This faith, this hope, this love – nothing can destroy.

Some years ago I had the great privilege of visiting the Holy Land. It was an unforgettable experience. Stories from the Bible that were so familiar came alive in a new way. To walk around the hills where Jesus walked and to cross the Sea of Galilee – almost unchanged since His day, was a moving adventure.

The Past and Present Meet

Standing out in the fields of Bethlehem where the shepherds heard the angels sing to announce the birth of Christ brought the story in the Gospel suddenly alive.

In the towns and cities it is sometimes harder to feel the atmosphere of Biblical times. The rush and bustle of everyday life can obscure the ancient truths. Nearly two thousand years of building over well-known sites can quickly hide their identity. Patient excavations, however, have laid bare many of the well-known sites of the Old and New Testaments. With a little imagination you can easily re-live the familiar stories from Biblical times, almost expecting to meet Abraham under the nearest tree or to bump into Peter around the next corner.

The Garden Tomb

For me one of the most moving moments was the visit we paid to the Garden Tomb. It is outside the old city of Jerusalem. In a beautiful garden with an atmosphere of deep peace we were shown around an empty tomb exactly like the one in which the body of Jesus was laid after His crucifixion on Calvary.

'Jesus is Alive To-day'

I shall never forget what our Arab Christian guide said to us that morning. He said: "We are not certain whether it was here or in some other place that Jesus Christ rose from the dead on that first Easter Day. The place is not all that important. What is important is that I know to-day Jesus is alive and I can talk to Him as my Saviour and my friend."

Sometime after I returned home I heard that that Arab Christian guide was one of the first to die in the so-called "Six day war" between the Arabs and the Jews. I know he was ready to meet the Lord he loved and with whom he talked each day.

At an early age I was introduced to the catechism of the Church of Ireland. I used to think the first question in that catechism was very odd. It simply asked: "What is your name?" and then suggested you answer "Christian name or names".

I used to think: "Why should someone who already knows who I am want to ask me that question". Over the years, however, I have come to realize how important that question is to me. The most important thing for me is to know who I am; to know that I was made in the image of God; to know that from all eternity God set His love upon me and desires that I should respond fully to that love.

'A Real Nowhere Man'

We hear so many people talk about 'a crisis of identity'. It is a real problem. That feeling of a lost generation was well expressed by a Beatles song a few years ago.

"He's a real nowhere man
Making all his nowhere plans for nobody
Doesn't have a point of view
Knows not where he's going to
Isn't he a bit like me and you?"

God Has Made You for Himself

My greatest need is to know who I am as a child of God; to know that when I come to Christ in repentance and faith and I put my trust in Him then my whole life takes on a new direction and purpose. You and I were not created to drift aimlessly through life like the 'nowhere man' of the Beatles song.

When God made you He did not make a mistake. He has a purpose and a plan for each life and the most important thing is to find that purpose and live in it. St Augustine as a young man was drifting aimlessly through life until one day he was confronted by the living Christ and in that personal encounter of faith his life was changed. Reflecting on his life he once said: *"God has made us for Himself and our hearts are restless till they find rest in Him."*

Ponder these words from St Paul in Romans 12 vs. 1 & 2:

"I appeal to you therefore, brethren, by the mercies of God, to present your bodies as a living sacrifice, holy and acceptable to God, which is your spiritual worship. Do not be conformed to this world but be transformed by the renewal of your mind, that you may prove what is the will of God, what is good and acceptable and perfect."

If you take St Paul's advice right now you will know who you are and where you're going.

John was a young boy who lived near the sea. During the winter he had spent long hours making a toy boat. In the early spring when he had it completed he proudly carried it to the shore. He successfully launched the boat. It gave him great joy as its little white sail caught the breeze and it bobbed up and down with the ebbing tide.

The tragedy struck. A large wave took John's little boat beyond his reach. Soon it was moving further out to sea. John watched helplessly as it moved further and further away. With a heavy heart he trudged home never expecting to see his little boat again.

Weeks later John was gazing into the window of one of the little shops in his village. The window was filled with all sorts of interesting things, fishermen's tackle and gear. And there right in the middle of the window was John's little boat. It looked damaged and the paint was badly scratched. But there was no doubt in John's mind – it was his boat, the one he had spent so many patient hours making.

Worth Everything

Without a moment's hesitation he went into the shop. Excitedly John explained to the man about his boat. But the man said: "A fisherman came in here a few days ago and I bought that boat from him. He found it in the sea. If you want it you will have to pay a pound for it." John rushed home to count his savings.

A pound was all he had. Without a further thought he raced back to the shop, handed over the pound and his precious boat was in his hands again.

Double Worth

With overflowing joy John held his boat and said: You're mine now twice over. I made you and I bought you."

That's what God has done for you and me. He not only created you but on the cross in Christ he redeemed you. He bought you back and you are His twice over.

"YOU ARE A V.I.P."

We were three hours flying time out from South Africa. Our plane was circling the island of Mauritius. It is a beautiful island set like a jewel in the midst of the glorious blue of the Indian Ocean. We had just touched down at Plaisance Airport when a call came for me over the intercom. I was asked to report to the Cabin Steward as I left the aircraft.

I was told to go to the V.I.P. lounge at the airport. Somewhat taken aback I went down the steps where I was met by another steward and escorted to the V.I.P. lounge where my distinguished host, Archbishop Trevor Huddleston was waiting to greet me.

God's Personal Love

On my travels abroad I had never been treated as a V.I.P. before. I got to thinking about that. I realized that God wants to treat each one of us as a Very Important Person. We are equally precious in His eyes. He took as much trouble to create you and me as He did to create the most distinguished people who ever lived. When Jesus died on the Cross He had each one of us in His heart. He cares for us that personally. He longs that we should know that in our experience and respond in joyful thanksgiving.

God's Estimate or Ours

So many of us spend time decrying ourselves. We think we are useless and worthless. That's not God's estimate of you and me. From all eternity He set His love upon us. In great love He created us and in great love He redeemed us. We are precious in His eyes and honoured and He loves us with an everlasting love.

As you read these words you may be feeling of little worth. Others, even your closest friends may have despaired of you. Are you going to believe your estimate or God's.

His Image can be Restored

Again and again Jesus made it clear both in His teaching and in His ministry to people that every man is created in God's image. However much that image has been defaced when we truly turn to God He can restore that image. However far we may have wandered He waits to welcome us home.

Fearfully and Wonderfully Made

Listen to these words from Psalm 139 and realize that in God's eyes you too are a V.I.P.

"For thou didst form my inward parts, thou didst knit me together in my mother's womb. I praise thee, for thou are fearful and wonderful. Wonderful are thy works! Thou knowest me right well; my frame was not hidden from thee, when I was being made in secret, intricately wrought in the depths of the earth. Thy eyes beheld my unformed substance; in thy book were written, every one of them, the days that were formed for me, when as yet there was none of them. How precious to me are thy thoughts, O God! How vast is the sum of them!"

Psalm 139 vs. 13-17

"HANDS"

Little Mary often wondered why her mother's hands were so ugly. One day she picked up the courage to ask her Mum why her hands were so different from others. Her mother took Mary on her knee and explained: "One day", Mum said, "when you were very small, and had just begun to crawl I was out of the room when you went too near the fire. I rushed into the room when I heard your screams. Your clothes were ablaze. I picked you up and quickly pulled the burning clothes off your body before you could be harmed. As I did so my hands were badly burned and I had to have long treatment in the hospital. I'm afraid, Mary, my hands will remain like that for the rest of my life."

The Most Beautiful Hands in the World

With tears in her eyes little Mary took her Mum's hands in hers and kissed them. Looking into her mother's face she said: "Mother, you have the most beautiful hands in the whole world".

The blessed hands of Jesus were wounded for you and me. Hands that touched the lepers and made them whole. Hands that touched blind eyes and made them see. Hands that raised men from death to life were wounded on the cross. Jesus allowed His hands to be nailed to that cruel cross because His heart was full of love for all men. The only thing in Heaven made by men's hands are the nail prints in the hands of Jesus.

Take His Hand

Those nail pierced hands reach out to-day to draw us back to God. Wherever you are as you read these words you can reach out to the risen Lord Jesus Christ and trust Him to take you by the hand and lead you home.

> *"I sometimes think about the Cross*
> *And shut my eyes and try to see*
> *The cruel nails and crown of thorns*
> *And Jesus crucified for me.*
>
> *But even could I see Him die*
> *I could but see a little part*
> *Of that great love which like a fire*
> *Is ever burning in His heart."*

"MEN DIE AS THEY LIVE"

Norman Williams is one of the very few survivors of the world's worst aircraft disaster. There were 653 passengers and crew on two Jumbo jets that collided on the ground in Teneriffe airport in March 1977. Only sixty people survived.

Nothing Short of a Miracle

Norman Williams described his escape from that terrible disaster as 'nothing short of a miracle.' Most of those who survived were in the front of the plane. Very few survived from the centre portion where he was. As the cabin of the aircraft burned like a furnace and filled with smoke the scene became one of indescribable horror.

In the Hour of Death

Williams recalls those awful moments before he was able to scramble through the burning inferno and jump clear. His words amazed and frightened me. "In the midst of this inferno, I could hear agonizing cries for help mingled with loud cursing as people burned to death. It shocked me to hear cursing because I thought if people were facing death they'd automatically call on God. *From this experience, I now believe that people die as they live.* If in their life they have been blasphemers, they will blaspheme in the time of disaster and death."

Words of Strength

Williams, who has been a committed Christian since he was a young man, explained how in those terrifying moments portions of Scripture flashed through his mind.
"I WILL NEVER LEAVE YOU NOR FORSAKE YOU", "I AM THE GOD WHO WILL DELIVER YOU" and "I AM THE SAME YESTERDAY, TODAY AND FOREVER."

Two Warnings

As I read the story of that terrible disaster there were two important warnings that came to me. First that this moment now is my moment of preparation for death. None of us knows the day or the hour that that call may come. No one can refuse that appointment.

"People die as they live."

The second is the need to store God's Word in our minds so that when disaster strikes we can recall God's unfailing promises.

When You Walk Through the Fire

Norman Williams tells how these wonderful words of Isaiah 43 came to his mind and gave him supernatural strength to escape from "his hell upon earth."

> *"But now thus says the Lord, he who created you, O Jacob, he who formed you, O Israel: 'Fear not, for I have redeemed you; I have called you by name, you are mine. When you pass through the waters I will be with you; and through the rivers, they shall not overwhelm you; when you walk through fire you shall not be burned, and the flame shall not consume you."*

Isaiah 43 vs. 1 & 2

A NEW CREATION

When I try to explain how God can renew our lives I often use an illustration out of the Old Testament – out of a book that few people probably read – the Book of Jeremiah. There's a fascinating little story in Chapter 18 of Jeremiah about a Potter. Jeremiah was a very sensitive person who almost despaired of his people's unfaithfulness to God – the people of Israel time and time again had turned away from God, and Jeremiah wondered what the end could be.

The Potter's Wheel

God spoke to him one day and gave him a strange message. *"Jeremiah, go down to the Potter's house"*. We can follow Jeremiah in our imagination as he made his way down the streets of Jerusalem to the Potter's shop. He entered the little door and before him on the counter and on the shelves sat the vessels that the Potter had just made. At the back of the shop the Potter was sitting at his wheel. Jeremiah joined him and watched intently as the Potter turned the wheel and moulded the clay with skilful hands. As Jeremiah watched, suddenly the clay broke in the Potter's hands. Instead of throwing the broken clay away the Potter took it and cast the same clay once more on the wheel and remoulded it, and re-made it, until he had it exactly as he wanted it. Then when he was satisfied he put it in the kiln to be fired, to take its place along side the other vessels for sale.

In a flash the message came home to Jeremiah – God was saying *"Cannot I do with Israel as the Potter has done with the clay."*

Lord, I am Willing

And I believe this is an illustration of how God deals with us as individuals. He does not cast us away when we break in His hands on the turning wheels of life. But he can remake us and renew us into the kind of people He wants us to be – on one condition – that we are willing.

Whatever may be the failure on your part God wants to restore to you the beauty of His creation. He can take you with all your sin and weakness and when you place yourself unreservedly in His strong hands He can make something beautiful with your life.

The Glory of God

"New every morning is the love
Our wakening and uprising prove;
Through sleep and darkness safely brought,
Restored to life, and power, and thought."

Dawn is a glorious moment in God's creation. It speaks of freshness, a new beginning and all the potential of a new day opening up before us.

I shall always treasure the memory of a new day dawning in the heart of Africa. I was with some friends in a game reserve right out in the bush. We had spent the night near a river that was teeming with wild life. The eerie stillness was only broken from time to time by the rumblings of the crocodiles and the croaking of the frogs. With the approach of dawn the stillness grew more intense and the air seemed filled with expectancy.

Suddenly over the dark horizon a glorious sun burst across the face of Africa. It is quite impossible to describe the grandeur of that moment that recalls the birth of the world. In the sun's rays a new day was born and all living things awoke to greet the dawn.

Love That is New Every Morning

In the wonder of that moment of God's re-creation of a new day there is hope for a fresh start for you and me. To-day can be for you the first day of the rest of your life. I find it very moving that it was in the very midst of great sorrow and sadness that the writer of the book of Lamentations could write these words:

"THE STEADFAST LOVE OF THE LORD NEVER CEASES,
HIS MERCIES NEVER COME TO AN END;
THEY ARE NEW EVERY MORNING; GREAT IS THY FAITHFULNESS."

Lamentations 3 vs. 22 & 23

Walk in the Light of God's Love

Only the light of the sun can dispel the darkness of the night. Only the light of Christ shining into my life can bring light and hope for this new day of God's appointment. Praise God for that light that He has given you for yet another day. Walk in that light. Allow the warm beams of His light to enter into every recess of your being to restore your life.

"THOSE WHO WISH TO SING ALWAYS
FIND A SONG"

I came across a lovely greeting card the other day. It pictured a
happy little bird hanging upside down from the branch of a tree.
Underneath were the words of a Swedish proverb:
"THOSE WHO WISH TO SING ALWAYS FIND A SONG"

"Te Deum"

I was reminded of one of the oldest and best known hymns in
the Christian Church. It is the "TE DEUM LAUDAMUS"

"We praise thee, O God: we acknowledge thee to be the Lord.
All the earth doth worship thee: the Father everlasting.
To thee all Angels cry aloud: the Heavens, and all the Powers
therein.
To thee Cherubin, and Seraphin: continually do cry,
Holy, Holy, Holy, Lord God of Sabaoth;
Heaven and earth are full of the Majesty, of thy glory."

It is said that this lovely hymn to God's glory was first sung at
St Augustine's baptism service. Filled with the spirit of joy and
adoration it is said that St Ambrose and St Augustine were
spontaneously inspired to sing this song verse about. It certainly
comes down from the earliest days of the Christian Church and
has inspired many with its majestic praise to God the Creator of
all things.

You Were Made to Praise

"Heaven and earth are full of the majesty, of thy glory" they
sang. The golden sunset and the delicate petals of the rose
equally reflect that glory of a Creator of infinite love and care.

The trees of the forest waving in the breeze offer a silent
praise. The waves of the sea crashing against the cliffs offer
their noisy praise. All creation rightly gives God praise. But to
man the choice is given. I may praise my Maker or remain
silent before the beauty of His creation. You too were made to
praise Him with the life He has given to you and which He
sustains in you in every moment of your existence.

"GOD'S MULTI-COLOURED NEW CREATION"

Behind the Christian Renewal Centre at Rostrevor the wooded slopes of the mountains of Mourne reach down to the water's edge. From early Spring till late Autumn those hillsides are a blaze of colour. The constantly changing patterns in the ancient oak forest blend with the varied shades of evergreens that command the upper slopes.

A People for God's Praise

For me it provides a vivid picture of what God is doing with His church in the world to-day. He is not producing a dull monochrome. In the Rostrevor forest which is part of His creation the different trees offer Him their silent praise. He wants to reflect with even greater glory the infinite variety of His "new creation", the Church as He gathers a people for His praise out of 'every tongue and people and nation.'

I have seen this great reality in many parts of the world as God's people discover their identity as His children. God did not make us all alike; it would be a dull world if He had done. What He wants, though, is not the clash of varied colours but their harmony as they blend together in one unison of praise.

The Harmonious Blend of Colour in South Africa

I saw this so vividly demonstrated when I had the privilege of addressing six thousand people at the South African Christian Leadership Assembly in Pretoria. I said then to those who were gathered there that there was hardly another country in the world that could provide such a demonstration of God's "multi-coloured new creation". Men and women were there from so many different tribes and colours. Their praise and worship were blending with Heaven where round the Throne day and night they never cease to sing!

> "Holy, holy, holy, is the Lord God Almighty,
> who was and is and is to come!
> Worthy art thou, our Lord and God, to receive
> glory and honour and power, for thou didst
> create all things, and by thy will they
> existed and were created."

Revelation 4 vs. 8b & 11

46

Wild-life films fascinate me. I saw one recently on T.V. about animal and bird life in a remote area of Australia. The region, near the coast of the Great Barrier Reef is severely flooded every year. I was intrigued by the ways the animals and insects adapt to cope with such an apparent calamity.

Conquering Fear

The ingenuity of a species of spiders particularly interested me. As the waters rise and the floods swell these spiders climb to the tops of the trees just above the flood line. There they spin marvellous silk veils where they can shelter from the waters below.

Like a fleet of ships in full sail their woven veils hang over the swollen waters; such delicate beauty conquering the fear of the water filled desert below.

As I watched how nature had provided for the protection of these tiny creatures I reflected on how God wants us to react in similar circumstances. All that those spiders needed for their protection they already had within them. What they had to do was put their plan into action.

A Place of Safety

For everyone who trusts in Jesus as his Saviour and his Lord there is a place of safety in His constant love and care. Down the centuries of time countless millions of men and women have proved in their own experience the truth of the words the Psalmist wrote several thousand years ago. Whatever storm is raging around you; whatever flood may threaten to engulf you, reach out to Jesus as you allow these words to strengthen your soul.

We Will Not Fear

"God is our refuge and strength, a very present help in trouble. Therefore we will not fear though the earth should change, though the mountains shake in the heart of the sea; though its waters roar and foam, though the mountains tremble with its tumult. There is a river whose streams make glad the city of God, the holy habitation of the Most High. God is in the midst of her, she shall not be moved; God will help her right early." Psalm 46 vs. 1-5

Rostrevor is set in one of the most beautiful parts of Ireland. The wooded slopes of the Mournes provide a backdrop of exquisite beauty for the village and the wide expanse of Carlingford Lough mirrors the splendour of the surrounding hills.

Beauty in Creation

Daily before our very eyes we see God's handiwork in the wonder of His creation. Before we came to live here we had spent eleven happy years in the centre of Belfast. One of the first things that struck me about Rostrevor was the sky. In the city, moving between tall buildings, I hardly noticed the sky. Here I can see the sky in its myriad moods; an ever changing panorama whose strokes of light and shade could scarcely be captured by the best landscape artist.

The night sky is equally beautiful, especially when the full moon spreads its beams across the still water of the Lough. Standing under the vault of heaven I can appreciate more fully the words of the Psalmist, when he reflected on the same scene several thousand years ago in Psalm 19:

> *"The heavens are telling the glory of God; and the firmament proclaims his handiwork. Day to day pours forth speech, and night to night declares knowledge. There is no speech, nor are there words; their voice is not heard; yet their voice goes out through all the earth, and their words to the end of the world."*

Open Your Eyes

John Calvin once said: *"Creation is the theatre of God's glory"*. There God speaks to us if we have eyes to see and ears to hear. Take time to see God in His handiwork and praise Him for His infinite love – for the beauty of earth and sea and sky and for the wonderful wisdom by which He has made them all.

Once I was teaching a class of eight year olds. We were thinking about the importance of saying 'Thank you'. I asked the children to tell me things that we should thank God for. All hands went up and the answers came thick and fast.

"We should thank God for our Mums and Dads, for brothers and sisters, for homes, for Church, for friends." Some even suggested we should thank God for school and teachers! Then some of the children began to suggest many things that make life easier for us. They said: "We should thank God for cars and planes, for washing machines . . ." and they added a host of other things.

Thank God for Jesus

Soon all the hands in the class were down. I thought they had exhausted all the things they wanted to thank God for. I was going to continue when suddenly, in the middle of the room a little boy shot his hand up and said: "Please Sir, we should thank God for Jesus." I thought 'how wonderful.'

I wonder if you have ever stopped to thank God for Jesus? Have you taken the time to turn to Him and thank Him from the bottom of your heart that He came into this world to bring you back from sin and give you a new life?

A General Thanksgiving

That little boy and his friends were expressing in their own simple and excited way what is expressed so beautifully in an ancient and familiar thanksgiving from the Book of Common Prayer:

"We thank you for our creation, preservation and all the blessings of this life; but above all for your inestimable love in the redemption of the world through our Lord Jesus Christ; for the means of grace and for the hope of glory."

Think on These Things:

"Know that the Lord is God! It is he that made us, and we are his; we are his people, and the sheep of his pasture. Enter his gates with thanksgiving, and his courts with praise! Give thanks to him, bless his name! For the Lord is good; his steadfast love endures for ever, and his faithfulness to all generations." Psalm 100 vs. 3-5

The Greatest is Love

LOVE IS STRONGER THAN HATE

"I love Idi Amin" is the unusual title of a book written by Bishop Festo Kivengere, the Anglican Bishop of Kigesi in Uganda.

Some time ago I had the opportunity to share in a week's Conference with Bishop Festo. He is a remarkable man. Though he bears the marks of deep suffering he radiates a joy that is rooted firmly in an unshakable faith in the risen Christ. At the height of Amin's terrible regime in 1977 Bishop Festo and his wife escaped across the border to neighbouring Ruanda. With only hours to spare they missed the sentence of death which had cut short the life of their dear friend and colleague Archbishop Luwum.

The Suffering Church in Uganda

Bishop Festo had lived through the experience of one of the most brutal dictatorships in modern history. Thousands of Christians in Uganda had been tortured and killed. Tens of thousands had to flee the country. It was with a very heavy heart that Bishop Festo left his homeland. Through his exile however he was spared to call millions of people all over the world to prayer for Uganda and he was able to share over the past few years in a remarkable ministry of reconciliation all over the world.

Naturally he had to wrestle with the thoughts of hatred towards Amin which stirred in his heart. He found an antidote to that hatred in the love of Christ.

Early in his exile he was in London. It was Good Friday and he made his way to All Souls' Church next to the B.B.C. For three hours he sat through a service of meditation reflecting on the cross of Christ. As he pondered again those immortal words of Christ on the Cross: *"Father forgive them; for they know not what they do"*. God spoke to him.

"Immediately there was as it were a great searchlight in my heart. Amin came into the picture, and the Lord said, 'You owe Amin forgiveness'. Sitting in All Souls' Church, London, I was stunned.

'But Lord, I don't hate this man.' The Lord said, 'Wait a minute. You have been growing hard towards him. Your attitude has been stiffening. Amin is not the loser – you are, Festo.'

It was quite a shock. Then the Lord said, 'You think it's hard to forgive him? Suppose when the soldiers were putting the nails into my hands, one of them had been President Amin. Would I have said, 'Father, forgive them all except Amin?' It was enough for Festo. In silence he bowed his head. Forgiveness and love entered in."

Love will Heal the Wounds of Time

Bishop Festo is now back in Uganda leading his people along the path of the reconciling love of Christ. It is not easy but he knows that it is the only way. Recently he wrote: *"It is a new day for the Kingdom in Uganda for now everywhere one goes, one meets thousands of young people, old people, sitting drinking in the Word. It is a very challenging time indeed and yet Uganda has inherited a terrible heritage from Amin. For eight years a new generation of our people knew nothing but murder, looting, false accusation, torture and most brutal experiences almost to the extent that the younger generation of 16 and 17 year olds think that the only way to settle matters between two people is to kill. Then to add to that there is bitterness in the hearts of many. Deep hurts which were caused when loved ones were taken away and brutally murdered do leave behind deep wounds in life ... The tendency under such circumstances is to fall for revenge – to 'get even', as they put it. This terrible poison needs an antidote; and so on our side there is a most exciting opportunity to preach the message of God's reconciling love. This is the only medicine for these horrible experiences. We have seen many turning to Him with tears of repentance. There is a need for restitutions, people who looted are now carrying burdens in their hearts. But this is where the Gospel comes in and we want to tell them of Jesus and His love. It is that love alone that can remove all the rubbish and bring back precious people for whom Christ died."*

FATHER FORGIVE

I have been reading "The Hard Awakening". It is written by the Bishop of Iran and tells the story of the last tragic years of that country and the suffering of Christians there. Miraculously the Bishop survived an assassination attempt on his life. Gunmen burst into his bedroom and his wife was wounded saving his life.

To Witness to His Love

I find it truly amazing that even after all the suffering he went through the Bishop could write: *"The power to suffer hardship, persecution and martyrdom was granted to us by God and we thank Him for counting us worthy to witness to His love"*.

Added to his own great suffering he received the news of the death of his own son, Bahram. On his way home from college, Bahram was kidnapped and cruelly murdered by terrorists. News of the death of his only son nearly broke the Bishop's heart. He prayed: *"O God the only thing which keeps us sane is our faith in your way: The way that life comes through death. The growth of a seed when it dies. Resurrection after Good Friday"*.

The day before Bahram's funeral the Bishop wrote this remarkable prayer. There are so many sad hearts in this land who can identify with these words. May they too be given that super-natural power to love that only comes from Christ.

"O God,
> *We remember not only Bahram but also his murderers;*
> *Not because they killed him in the prime of his youth*
> *and made our hearts bleed and our tears flow,*
> *Not because with this savage act they have brought*
> *further disgrace on the name of our country among*
> *the civilized nations of the world;*
> *But because through their crime we now follow thy*
> *footsteps more closely in the way of sacrifice.*
> *The terrible fire of this calamity burns up all*
> *selfishness and possessiveness in us;*
> *Its flame reveals the depth of depravity and meanness*
> *and suspicion, the dimension of hatred and the measure*
> *of sinfulness in human nature;*
> *It makes obvious as never before our need to trust in*
> *God's love as shown in the cross of Jesus and his resurrection;*
> *Love which makes us free from hate towards our persecutors;*

*Love which brings patience, forbearance, courage, loyalty,
     humility, generosity, greatness of heart;
Love which more that ever deepens our trust in God's
     final victory and his eternal designs for the Church and for the
          world;
     Love which teaches us how to prepare ourselves to face our own
          day of death.
O God,
Bahram's blood has multiplied the fruit of the Spirit in the soil of
     our souls;
     So when his murderers stand before thee on the day of judgement
     Remember the fruit of the Spirit by which they have enriched our
          lives,
     And forgive."*

55

"THE GREATEST FORCE IN THE WORLD"

The greatest force in all the world is the power of forgiving love. From the cross of Calvary Jesus Christ prayed for those who had hung Him there. Even as they mocked Him, and spat on Him He called out to His Heavenly Father: "FORGIVE THEM".

Down the ages since then men and women have been inspired by the Spirit of Christ to do that which is humanly impossible – to forgive those who have deeply wronged them.

Senseless Cruelty

Over the past twelve years of violence and destruction in Northern Ireland I have been deeply moved to see that Spirit expressed in the lives of many who have been wounded and bereaved by the senseless cruelty of their fellow men.

Mrs Cobb was one of those touched by the Spirit of Christ's forgiving love in a remarkable way. In 1977 she was left a widow when her husband, a police inspector was murdered by an I.R.A. gunman.

Praying for Forgiveness

One of those who took part in the Maze hunger strike was convicted of that murder. Two weeks before Christmas Florence Cobb wrote a letter to that man in prison to tell him that she forgave him for the murder of her husband. "I feel no bitterness", she said. "I am praying for the man who killed my husband. I am praying that he will find God's forgiveness and come to know Jesus as His Saviour and Lord."

Forgiving Love

I am convinced that that act of forgiving love had great power to break the grip of evil that threatened the peace of Christmas in this land. Only through that love can this land be released from the demonic power that would plunge us into even worse disaster.

It was St Paul who himself was converted from a life of bigotry and bitterness who once wrote:

"Repay no one for evil . . . Beloved, never avenge yourselves, but leave it to the wrath of God; Do not be overcome by evil, but overcome evil with good." Romans 12 vs. 17, 19 & 21.

Over the past twelve years in Northern Ireland something which has constantly inspired and humbled me has been the courage of those who have had to suffer terrible injury and tragic bereavement. Often those who have suffered most have been most ready to forgive.

Murder and Sudden Death

Meta was one of those. It was during a Conference at the Christian Renewal Centre that she came and asked some of us to pray with her. Only a week before, her brother, a policeman had been ambushed and brutally killed by terrorists when he and his colleagues came to investigate a false report of a break-in at a garage in Warrenpoint. Meta had loved her brother very dearly and the grief she felt was intense.

The Lonely Road to Forgiveness

Meta had now travelled that same road which her brother had gone that fatal night. She said: "My heart was filled with bitterness and hatred for those who had carried out this attack. As a Christian I knew this was not right, yet despite knowing this I could not help myself. A friend suggested I should pray for the gunmen but at this time that seemed impossible. How could I pray for someone who had killed my brother?"

The Miracle of Forgiveness

As we prayed the miracle happened. Some time later I heard Meta speak to a group of people from all over Ireland. With a remarkable calm and peace she said: As Christian brothers and sisters laid hands on me and prayed with me, in a wonderful way the love of God filled my heart and I received a great peace. I could pray and say: "Father, forgive them."

The Power to Love

That is the power to love that only Jesus Christ can give and it's the power that you and I need so much in this hour of Ireland's crisis. It is the power that is stronger than the power of hate that plants a bomb or the power of fear that pulls a trigger – Jesus' power – the power to love.

Battle, murder and sudden death fill the daily headlines of the world. Men's hearts fail them for fear of what is coming on the earth.

The Bible has no illusions about the battle we are in. It is a battle of good against evil, of darkness against light. Jesus knew it was a battle that rages in the heart of every man. He said: "Light has come into the world but men love darkness rather than light because their deeds are evil."

Hate or Love

I once met a young man in prison who illustrated this in a vivid way. Tattooed on the fingers of his left hand he had the letters H A T E and on the fingers of his right hand L O V E! I said to him: "What's your choice going to be? You can't have both in the same body. And you have to make a choice."

Put up Your Sword

In a moment of great danger Jesus and His disciples had to make that choice. You remember in the Garden of Gethsemane when Jesus was surrounded by the mob who came to arrest Him Peter drew his sword and injured the servant of the high priest. Jesus already knew that only by the way of love could the world be won. Instantly He healed the injured man. The words of rebuke He spoke to Peter echo down the centuries and come with telling urgency into the situation in our land to-day.

"Put your sword back in its place," Jesus said to him, *"for all who take the sword will perish by the sword."*

The Pope's Appeal

When the news broke of the cruel attack on Pope John Paul's life the world was stunned but sadly not surprised. Violence seems endemic now. When I heard the news I turned again to what the Pope had said about violence when he spoke in Ireland.

Pray to God that these words of wisdom will no longer go unheeded in this land of ours.

Turn From Violence

"Now I wish to speak to all men and women engaged in violence. I appeal to you, in language of passionate pleading.

On my knees I beg you to turn away from the paths of violence and to return to the ways of peace. You may claim to seek justice. I, too, believe in justice and seek justice. But violence only delays the day of justice. Violence destroys the work of justice. Further violence in Ireland will only drag down to ruin the land you claim to love and the values you claim to cherish. In the name of God I beg you: return to Christ, who died so that men might live in forgiveness and peace. He is waiting for you, longing for each one of you to come to Him so that He may say to each of you: your sins are forgiven; go in peace."

Love Life

"I appeal to young people who may have become caught up in organisations engaged in violence. I say to you, with all the love I have for you, with all the trust I have in young people: do not listen to voices which speak the language of hatred, revenge, retaliation. Do not follow any leaders who train you in the ways of inflicting death. Love life, respect life; in yourselves and in others. Give yourself to the service of life, not the work of death. Do not think that courage and strength are proved by killing and destruction. The true courage lies in working for peace. The true strength lies in joining with the young men and women of your generation everywhere in building up a just and human and Christian society by the ways of peace. Violence is the enemy of justice. Only peace can lead the way to true justice."

More than Conquerors

As the message of Christ spread in the early Church men and women from every race turned to Christ in faith and obedience. Again and again that faith was tested on the anvil of persecution. First it was the prejudice and bitterness of the Jews which fanned the flames of hatred. Later the Christians had to face the might of the Roman Empire. To be a loyal member of the Roman Empire you were required to offer your total allegiance to Caesar, often to the extent of acknowledging him as God.

The Day of Testing

For those who had put their faith in Jesus Christ as Lord the day of testing came when at the threat of death they were asked to confess: "Caesar is Lord." Some did this and took the way of compromise, avoiding physical torture and death. Thousands of other Christians in the first century and down through the succeeding centuries refused to give their primary allegiance to any other than Christ.

"Christ Has Never Done Me Wrong"

Polycarp was one of those. He was a leader in the Church of Smyrna, a city in Asia Minor, now Turkey. In the year 167 AD a fierce persecution broke out against the Christians. Polycarp was persuaded by his people to go into hiding. This he did where he remained in constant prayer for his persecuted friends. Soon however, his enemies designed a scheme to bring him out of hiding. They took as hostage a young child, who under torture revealed where Polycarp was.

He was brought back to the city of Smyrna where his persecutors tried every means to persuade him to give up his Christian faith. When he appeared in the Roman Amphitheatre the magistrate said to him: "Swear, curse Christ and I will set you free." The old man answered: "Eighty and six years have I served Christ and He has never done me wrong: how then can I curse my King and my Saviour?"

Worthy to Suffer for Christ

When he had withstood further threats the fatal proclamation was made, that "Polycarp confessed himself a Christian". He was condemned to be burnt alive. In rage his enemies hurried to prepare his place of execution. The old man took his place beside the stake. When they went to tie him he said to them. "Leave me unfastened; he who has enabled me to brave the fire will give strength also to endure its fierceness". Then he prayed: "O Lord, God Almighty, the Father of your beloved Son Jesus Christ, through whom we have received a knowledge of you, God of the Angels and of the whole creation, of the whole race of man, and of the Saints who live before your presence, I thank you that you have thought me worthy, this day and this hour, to share the cup of your Christ among the number of your witnesses."

The fire was kindled; but a high wind drove the flame to one side and prolonged his sufferings. Polycarp died in the faith that had sustained him through all the trials of his life.

The Crown of Life

A few years before St John the Divine had written these words to the Christians in Symrna. No doubt they were a source of strength to Polycarp in that fatal moment of trial:

"The words of the first and the last, who died and came to life. 'I know your tribulation and your poverty (but you are rich) and the slander of those who say that they are Jews and are not, but are a synagogue of Satan. Do not fear what you are about to suffer. Behold, the devil is about to throw some of you into prison, that you may be tested, and for ten days you will have tribulation. Be faithful unto death, and I will give you the crown of life."

Revelation 2 vs. 8-10

Hope seems to be in short supply in our world to-day. We see all around us so many seemingly hopeless situations and there are many counsels to despair.

The Christian can never share the world's despair. God gives His people hope even in the midst of despair. He is Lord and nothing in all creation can separate us from His love. The hope He gives is that beyond death there is life. In the trials and tribulations He is my rock and my fortress.

> *"Because He lives I can face to-morrow*
> *Because He lives all fear is gone*
> *Because I know He holds the future*
> *And life is worth the living just because He lives."*

Hope in a Nazi Prison

That hope has sustained Christians in every age through the most difficult circumstances.

During the last war there were many Germans who saw the awful evil in Hitler's regime. Among them was a well-known Christian theologian Dietrich Bonhoeffer. Towards the end of the war he was arrested and imprisoned because of his resolute stand against Hitler. He was condemned to death by the Nazis and executed on the 8th April, 1945.

A Living Hope in Christ

On the last day of his life he conducted a short service in his prison cell for the other prisoners. The text from which he preached were the words of St Peter in his first letter to the earliest Christians.

> *"Blessed be the God and Father of our Lord Jesus Christ! By his great mercy we have been born anew to a living hope through the resurrection of Jesus Christ from the dead, and to an inheritance which is imperishable, undefiled, and unfading, kept in heaven for you."*

1 Peter 1 vs. 3 & 4

'The End But Also the Beginning'

During the silence that followed the service the guards burst into the cell to take Bonhoeffer to his death. His last words were a message to his friend, Bishop Bell of Chichester, "Tell him", he said, "that for me this is the end, but also the beginning. With him I believe in the principle of our universal brotherhood which rises above all national interests and that our victory is certain."

Do Not Fear the Firebrands

Two years later another Christian pastor, Johannes Mickley, imprisoned by the communists in Russia wrote these words from his prison cell.

> "Take your heart in both hands when troubles frighteningly storm over you.
> Do not fear the firebrands – there is One who protects you.
> Know you are never deserted, grasp it, you are never alone.
> Even if all should forget you God will be near to you.
> He became like one of us, brother to us in suffering and death.
> And so He knows like no one else your struggles and your need.
> Bring your heart to Him, let Him fill it; come and take from His strength,
> All fear He will still and imprisonment become freedom."

Think on These Things

> "Commit your way to the Lord; trust in him, and he will act. He will bring forth your vindication as the light, and your right as the noonday. Be still before the Lord, and wait patiently for him; fret not yourself over him who prospers in his way, over the man who carries out evil devices!"
>
> Psalm 37 vs. 5-7

On the 23rd June, 1978 the world was shocked by the news of the atrocious massacre of nine missionaries with four of their children in Rhodesia. Most of them were serving together as teachers in a school at a place called Vumba on the border with Mozambique. As darkness fell on that June evening in that remote part of Africa terrorist guerillas came out of the bush, rounded up those defenceless men, women and children and within a few minutes thirteen more were added to the roll of Christian martyrs in Africa.

Wendy White was one of those who died. She was a good friend whom my wife and I had known since we were students together in Trinity College in Dublin. After taking her degree Wendy had trained as a Social worker and for some years worked in London. Her steady pursuit of a career was dramatically altered by a clear call from God. It happened when Wendy visited South Africa in 1973 and stayed at a number of mission hospitals. It was then that she re-dedicated her life to Christ to serve Him wherever He would call her.

For Me to Live is Christ

She returned to England where she gave up her social work and trained to be a nurse. After she had finished her nursing training Wendy came to visit us at the Christian Renewal Centre. As we talked and prayed together we recognized that she had a clear call from God to go to Rhodesia. She arrived there in 1977 and immediately began work as a nurse in a large school in one of the most dangerous areas of terrorist activity.

She was fully aware of the cost of her obedience to the Lord's call but she knew that her life was in God's hands and nothing, not even death could separate her from His love. A song which Wendy's friend recorded a few days before they both died summed up her resolve:

> *"For me to live is Christ*
> *To die is gain*
> *To hold His hand and walk His narrow way*
> *There is no peace no joy no thrill*
> *Like walking in His will*
> *For me to live is Christ*
> *To die is gain."*

A Love that Never Gives Up

When we received the tragic news of Wendy's murder we turned to the last letter she had written to us – it began: *"Loving Greetings to you in the precious Name of our Lord Jesus. He reigns in glory and is coming soon:"* and then she added a text from Isaiah 59 verse 19: *"When the enemy comes in like a flood, the Lord shall lift up a standard against him."*

She went on to thank those who had been praying for her: *"I really believe that we are labourers together,"* she wrote. *"Only the Saviour knows the lost sheep, but He wants our lips, hands, and feet to be ready and seek them, with Him. It is LOVE that never gives up, that believes all things and endures all things. Please pray that we may have His love in our hearts . . . I believe that is what we need above all else."*

Wendy ended her letter by encouraging us to read Psalm 46 and especially drew our attention to verses 10 and 11:

"Be still and know that I am God. I am exalted among the nations; I am exalted in the earth."

In her last letter she asked us also to pray for many young Christians in Rhodesia who were being asked by militant revolutionaries to renounce Christ. She said:

"In some places the real Christians are being strengthened in the face of persecution but very few 'stand' when asked to denounce the name of Jesus at the point of a gun."

And she added: – *"Would you?"*

In the gathering darkness of that June evening as the forces of evil moved in on that little community of Christians Wendy had to answer that question.

The last words that she spoke before she was shot were to one of her companions.

"They may kill our bodies but they cannot kill our souls".

Think on These Things:

"But I do not account my life of any value nor as precious to myself, if only I may accomplish my course and the ministry which I received from the Lord Jesus, to testify to the gospel of the grace of God."

Acts 20 v. 24

THE FIRST ZULU CHRISTIAN MARTYR

A simple cross on top of a high hill right in the heart of Zululand is an important landmark in the story of the Christian mission to Southern Africa. With many African Christians and missionaries from different parts of the world my wife and I climbed that hill. It was a unique privilege for us to share in that simple yet joyful and challenging service. It was held to mark the 104th anniversary of the martyrdom of Maqamusela Kanyile. On that spot in 1877 he chose death rather than deny his faith in Christ who had saved him and set him free from the bonds of darkness.

"I Choose Baptism"

Resentful of the white men's intrusion into his land, Cetshwayo, king of the Zulus, forbade any of his people to accept baptism from the missionaries. When it was reported to him that Maqamusela was being prepared for baptism, the king sent word that he should be given the opportunity to recant and, if he refused, that he should be put to death. Maqamusela was thus presented with the same choice as many Christians have had to face since the first days of the Church, and he gave the same answer to the king's men. 'I choose baptism.' When warned that they would have to kill him, he replied 'Very well, but please give me time to say my prayers, then kill me quickly and hurry home before the approaching thunderstorm breaks'. So died the first Christian martyr.

"Let Us Go and Serve the Lord"

Those who gathered there were encouraged to follow his example of steadfastness and courage and to carry the flame of faith across their land. We were welcomed from Ireland and those people held us in their prayers.

The service ended with a joyful song of commitment. "Let us go and serve the Lord." It echoed across the valleys of Zululand with its message of challenge and faith.

The Light of Life

Darkness was falling as we made our way down the hill. Yet I was aware of the great light that shone from that place. I remembered the words of Jesus: *"You are the light of the world. A city set on a hill cannot be hid."* And his words of promise that have never failed in any age or place.

"I AM THE LIGHT OF THE WORLD; HE WHO FOLLOWS ME WILL NOT WALK IN DARKNESS, BUT WILL HAVE THE LIGHT OF LIFE."

"In the world you have tribulation; but be of good cheer, I have overcome the world"

Those were the words of Jesus to His disciples before He was cruelly condemned and brutally put to death before their very eyes.

Persecution

Within a few short years the young Church was being subjected to fierce persecution. St Stephen, the first Christian martyr was stoned to death by a crowd of fanatical Jews who wanted to wipe out the followers of the "man from Galilee". One of those who gave his support to the terrible murder of Stephen was Saul of Tarsus. In the record of the Acts of the Apostles we are told that those who carried out the foul murder laid their clothes at the feet of a young man named Saul, who gave silent assent to his execution.

A Personal Encounter with Christ

That man, Saul of Tarsus became Paul, the greatest Christian missionary of all time! What brought about such a change? What was it that turned a man who was so full of prejudice and hatred into a great saint of the Church? We know from the account in the Acts of the Apostles that it was in a direct personal encounter with the living Lord Jesus Christ that Saul's life was radically and dramatically changed.

'Lord Forgive Them'

Yet I have no doubt that what Saul witnessed as he stood by while Stephen was stoned to death made an indelible impression on him. He could never be the same again as he watched the face of Stephen and how he reacted to the furious rage of those who battered him to death. We are told that as the rocks were hurled at Stephen "he was filled through all his being with the Holy Spirit". As the life ebbed from his broken body he called out in prayer to God and said: *"Lord, do not hold this sin against them."*

The Power of Love

What do you do in the face of faith and love like that? I am sure that moment was the beginning of Saul's conversion. That moment must have proved for Saul that love is stronger than hate and that blind prejudice and hatred is powerless in the face of such love. That love conquered Saul and changed him into Paul the great Apostle of Love. After years of suffering and persecution for his faith in Christ Paul wrote these words to the Christians at Rome.

Think on These Things:

"Rejoice in your hope, be patient in tribulation, be constant in prayer. Bless those who persecute you; bless and do not curse them. Repay no one evil for evil, but take thought for what is noble in the sight of all. If possible, so far as it depends upon you, live peaceably with all. Beloved, never avenge yourselves, but leave it to the wrath of God; for it is written, 'Vengeance is mine, I will repay, says the Lord.' No, 'if your enemy is hungry, feed him, if he is thirsty, give him drink; for by so doing you will heap burning coals upon his head."

Romans 12 vs. 12, 14, 17-20

70

Peace of Christ

THROUGH CLOUD AND SUNSHINE

Where we live on the shore of Carlingford Lough we are always aware of the constantly changing moods of the sky. Sometimes a deep mist creeps up the Lough and within a few minutes the mountains are blotted from view. At other times blankets of clouds roll across the hills, with the sun occasionally bursting through and like a great searchlight picking out the varied shades of green on the hills beyond.

The Mists of Doubt and Fear

The scene reminds me of our lives and the varied circumstances of joy and sorrow which we all pass through. Thousands of people have come to the Christian Renewal Centre since it was established seven years ago. Many times their lives have been clouded by deep sorrow or the mists of doubt and fear have crept over them robbing them of peace.

The Peace of Christ

Our ministry is to point them to Jesus, the Son of righteousness, with healing in His touch. Again and again we have seen Christ reach into the deepest problem in a human life and bring His deep inner peace and calm. It is only the perfect love of Christ that can cast out fear from our lives. You don't need to come to the beauty of Rostrevor to know that peace that passes human understanding. Jesus, the Prince of Peace is close to you now, nearer than you know. From all eternity He set His love upon you and He is drawing you to Himself, however far you may have wandered from Him.

The Shadows Flee Away

I came across this lovely blessing in a friend's home on the island of Mauritius. It touched my heart when I read it and I know it will bless you too. It was written by Fra Giovanni as long ago as 1513.

"No Heaven can come to us
Unless our heart find rest in to-day.
Take Heaven.
No Peace lies in the future which is not hidden
In this present little instant.
Take Peace.

72

The gloom of the world is but a shadow,
Behind it, yet within our reach, is joy.
There is radiance and glory in the darkness
Could we but see, and to see we have only to look
    I beseech you to look.

And so, at this time, I greet you.
Not quite as the world sends greetings,
But with profound esteem,
And with prayer that for you now and forever
The day breaks, and the shadows flee away."

"THE BLESSING OF PEACE"

"Deep peace of the Running Wave to you,
Deep peace of the Flowing Air to you,
Deep peace of the Quiet Earth to you,
Deep peace of the Shining Stars to you,
Deep peace of the Son of Peace to you."

That's an old Irish blessing which someone passed on to me last week. It came at a moment when I really needed that message.

The Prince of Peace

We long for peace in our troubled world. We pray for peace in our broken land. We desire peace in our hearts when all around us there is violence, bitterness and hatred. We can only have real peace when we allow the Prince of Peace to reign and rule in our hearts and lives. I cannot bring peace to others if I am myself a walking battlefield.

Peace in the Midst of Turmoil

The peace which Christ brings is a peace in the midst of turmoil. Jesus was under no illusions about the difficulties that His followers would face in a world that had rejected Him the Prince of Peace. He warned them: *"In the world you have tribulation; but be of good cheer, I have overcome the world."*

As I look around to-day I see people frantically trying to find some security in this passing world. Jesus knew better than any that man can find no lasting peace in things. Those who put their faith in Jesus Christ know that when everything else is taken from them they have the peace of His presence and a joy too deep for words.

Christ's Promise of Peace

Even now as you read these words allow the Lord Jesus Christ to minister His peace within your soul as you meditate on this promise which He first made to His disciples. It still holds good for you.

"PEACE I LEAVE WITH YOU; MY PEACE I GIVE TO YOU; NOT AS THE WORLD GIVES DO I GIVE TO YOU. LET NOT YOUR HEARTS BE TROUBLED, NEITHER LET THEM BE AFRAID."

St John 14 v. 27

"I WILL FEAR NO EVIL"

One of the great privileges of being a Christian pastor is that one is allowed to share in the most sacred moments of people's lives.

Joy and Sorrow

One day in the life of a minister can include a wide variety of shared human experiences. Joy shared with a family in the birth of a child; with a young couple in their marriage; with someone in the success of some achievement. That day may also bring the shared sorrow of family bereavement, sudden accidents or sickness.

Fortitude

In sharing these experiences of joy and sorrow with so many people over the years one impression always returns to me. I recall the inspiration that so many have been to me in those moments when all hope seemed gone. I recall the fortitude with which people have faced some terrible illness or tragedy and I have seen their faith grow stronger under such deep trials.

Peace

Eileen was one of those. All who knew her were inspired with confidence and joy as they witnessed her deep peace in the face of serious illness and great pain.

Shortly before she died Eileen sent us the words of a poem which sustained her during her final illness. I pass it on especially to those of you who are going through difficult times just now.

Confidence

"I will not ask to know the future years
Nor cloud to-day with dark to-morrow's fears
I will but ask a light from heaven to show
How, step by step, my pilgrimage should go.

And if the distant perils seem to make
The path impossible that I must take
Yet as a river winds through mountains lone
The way will open up as I go on.

75

> Be still my heart; for faithful is your Lord
> And pure and true and tried His Holy Word
> Through stormy flood that rages as the sea
> His promises like stepping stones should be."

Think on These Things:

"Even though I walk through the valley of the shadow of death, I fear no evil; for thou are with me; thy rod and thy staff, they comfort me."

Psalm 23 v. 4

David, a friend of mine was involved in a car accident. When he woke up in hospital his eyes were covered in bandages. He was told there was a danger that he might never see again. A verse of scripture came to him as a great comfort in those days and weeks. I'll pass it on to you. It may be just the message for you in the situation in which you find yourself today. The word is in Isaiah 26 verses 3 & 4:

> *"Thou dost keep him in perfect peace, whose mind is stayed on thee, because he trusts in thee. Trust in the Lord for ever, for the Lord God is an everlasting rock."*

The peace of God is not always an absence of conflict. It's a deep assurance of God's love in the midst of trouble. Here's how Jesus expressed it to his friends before His death.

> *"Peace I leave with you; my peace I give to you; not as the world gives do I give to you. Let not your hearts be troubled, neither let them be afraid."*

St John 14 v. 27

Just allow the truth of that promise to come to you wherever you are right now. Claim Christ's gift of peace which He longs to give you in this moment. It may help you to pray these words of John Whittier's hymn:

> *"Dear Lord and Father of mankind,*
> *Forgive our foolish ways;*
> *Re-clothe us in our rightful mind,*
> *In purer lives thy service find,*
> *In deeper reverence, praise.*
>
> *Drop thy still dews of quietness,*
> *Till all our strivings cease;*
> *Take from our souls the strain and stress,*
> *And let our ordered lives confess*
> *The beauty of thy peace."*

Instrument of His Peace

You cannot bring peace to others if you yourself are a walking battlefield. As you allow the peace of Christ to pervade your whole being you will be a channel of that precious gift to others.

Was there ever a time when this world and our land stood more in need of that peace that 'passes human understanding'?

Would you join a great army of peace in this land to pray with me that lovely prayer of St Francis:

"Lord, make me an instrument of your peace
Where there is hatred let me bring love
Where there is injury pardon
Where there is doubt faith
Where there is despair hope
Where there is darkness light
Where there is sadness joy
Grant that we may not seek so much to be consoled as to console;
to be understood as to understand; to be loved as to love; for it is
in giving that we receive, in pardoning we are pardoned and in
dying we are born to eternal life through Jesus Christ our Lord."

LIGHT IN THE DARKNESS

Some time ago we took our young sons to see a lighthouse on the Co. Down coast. It was a fascinating visit for us all.

The lighthouse keeper made us very welcome and gave us a most intriguing guided tour. He led us up the winding stairs until we reached the platform at the top. As we looked out to sea and across the rolling Co. Down countryside the view was breathtaking. But the lighthouse was not built to give visitors a view of the mountains and the sea. At the foot of that building there were rocks reaching out into the sea – a constant hazard to passing ships. The lighthouse was built to warn of danger.

Reflecting the Light

I had often seen the light from that particular lighthouse beaming out for miles around. What intrigued me as I stood there looking at that light was its smallness. The light that beamed out to pierce the darkness of the surrounding ocean was provided by a tiny gas mantle fed from a cylinder at the base of the lighthouse. But all around that tiny light were revolving glass prisms perfectly set to catch that light and reflect it out for miles around.

It was tempting to reach out to those glass prisms but the keeper warned us not to touch them. He explained that even a finger print on one of them could stain it and make it less effective in reflecting the light as it revolved around the little mantle in the centre.

Jesus – The Light of the World

That experience taught me two important lessons for our lives as Christians in the world. Jesus Christ is the "Light of the World" and it is only as we look at Him that we can reflect His light. Men and women who have lost their way in life and are in danger of being shipwrecked need to see the light of Christ in you and me.

We are like those glass prisms that revolve around the light. The light is not in us but in Christ. So many things in our lives can dim the reflexion of that light and make it harder for others to find their way to Him.

"Abide with me; fast falls the eventide;
  The darkness deepens; Lord, with me abide,
  When other helpers fail, and comforts flee,
  Help of the helpless, O abide with me."

Those words are the first verse of one of the best known hymns in the English language. For over one hundred years they have been sung all over the world. Whether sung by a small congregation in a country church or by tens of thousands on cup final day at Wembley the words have deeply touched the lives of millions of people.

Portora Royal School

Henry Francis Lyte who wrote this famous hymn was born in Scotland. His early childhood was not very happy and the loss of his mother whom he dearly loved was a great blow to him. The orphaned boy of seven became a pupil at Portora Royal School in Enniskillen where Dr Burrows, the Headmaster made it possible for him to complete his schooling. After taking his degree from Trinity College, Dublin Lyte was ordained into the ministry of the Church of Ireland and became rector of Taghmon in Co. Wexford.

A Personal Encounter with Christ

It was there, while ministering to a neighbouring rector who was dying that Henry Francis Lyte had a deep personal encounter with Christ that was to change the whole course of his life and ministry. What had been 'head knowledge' now became 'heart knowledge'. His writing and preaching took on new life and conviction, as he introduced people to the living Lord he knew so well.

Brixham – Final Illness

After a serious illness Lyte moved to minister in the South of England where until his death in 1847 he was vicar of Brixham, a fishing port on a beautiful part of the South English coast.

It was in the beauty of that place he wrote "Abide with me". As he looked out over the sea the wonder of the sunset reflected the sunset in his soul. He was suffering from a serious illness and he knew he had not long to live. *"I knew when I wrote that hymn it came from direct inspiration,"* he said. *"There were thick clouds overhead and the storm seemed about to break and the inspiration came upon me."*

"Swift to its close ebbs out life's little day,
Earth's joys grow dim its glories pass away.
Change and decay in all around I see
O Thou who changest not, abide with me.

Not a brief glance I beg, a passing word,
But as Thou dwellest with Thy disciples Lord,
Familiar, condescending, patient, free,
Come not to sojourn, but abide with me."

Nothing Terrible in Death

Soon after he wrote the hymn Henry Francis Lyte at the age of 54 passed on into the nearer presence of the Lord whom he loved. Before he died he spoke to the nurse: *"Oh there is nothing terrible in death, Jesus Christ steps down into the grave before me."* His last words were: *"Peace and joy"*. No doubt the final verse of his famous hymn was on his heart.

"Hold thou thy Cross before my closing eyes;
Shine through the gloom, and point me to the skies;
Heaven's morning breaks, and earth's vain shadows flee:
In life, in death, O Lord, abide with me."

81

'MARANATHA'

"MARANATHA – Come, Lord Jesus" was a frequent prayer in the early Church. It has echoed through the Church in every age and is being heard again with increasing frequency.

As Christ was parted from His disciples at the Ascension the promise was given that He would come again. As the puzzled disciples looked up two heavenly messengers were called to them:

"Men of Galilee, why do you stand looking into heaven? This Jesus, who was taken up from you into heaven, will come in the same way as you saw him go into heaven."

A Day of Joy

Sometime, we do not know the day or the hour that promise will be fulfilled. Christ will come again in glory and power to reign on the earth. That will be a day of great joy for all who are longing for His Kingdom to come on earth as it is in Heaven.

Without Warning

Jesus Himself said that day will come without warning; like a thief in the night; like a sudden flash of lightning. That is why He warned men to be ever ready, to be watchful and alert.

John Wesley was once asked: 'What would you do if you knew that the Lord would return to-day?' He's said to have answered: "I wouldn't change my plans!" How many of us could say the same?

Lo, He Comes

John Wesley's brother, Charles adapted a hymn written by John Cennick which expresses the longing of Christians for the second advent of their Lord.

"Lo! he comes; with clouds descending,
Once for favoured sinners slain;
Thousand thousand saints attending
Swell the triumph of his train;
Hallelujah!
God appears on earth to reign.

Those dear tokens of his Passion
Still his dazzling body bears,
Cause of endless exultation
To his ransomed worshippers:
With what rapture
Gaze we on those glorious scars!

Yea, Amen; let all adore thee,
High on thine eternal throne:
Saviour, take the power and glory;
Claim the kingdom for thine own,
Hallelujah!
Everlasting God, come down.   Amen."

Hope Beyond Despair

"The Power of the Cross" was the theme of a remarkable Conference held in Belfast. Up to 1,500 people from all over Ireland gathered. For two days Roman Catholics and Protestants praised God together, prayed together and shared God's Word together. They came in repentance to Christ, acknowledging that only through His death and resurrection can we be raised to new life.

A Germ of Hope

It was a moving experience to see people from such varied backgrounds acknowledge Jesus Christ as Lord. God by His Holy Spirit healed many deep seated prejudices and fears and made it possible for us truly to forgive one another.

In that gathered company of people I could see a germ of Ireland's only hope for peace. Only as Roman Catholics and Protestants come together to Christ and together acknowledge Him alone as Saviour and Lord can we speak peace to our divided land.

The Miracle of Reconciling Love

At the Cross Jesus Christ made this miracle possible. The vertical bar of the Cross speaks of the way in which Christ has reconciled me to the Father. When I come there in repentance and faith God forgives me and sets me free from all the guilt of the past. The horizontal bar speaks of that further reconciliation which Christ has made possible; He makes me friends with all those who have come there together with me.

No Barriers at the Cross

When as a sinner I come to the cross of Christ and find there His amazing love and mercy I am kneeling with others whom before I might have seen as enemies. I cannot refuse to call him brother whom my Father has made His son.

Someone who was at that Conference in Belfast reflected on the theme and wrote these words. I pass them on for your meditation.

THE CROSS

Symbol of God's glory
Symbol of hope in the dark
Of triumph over sin and death
Symbol of love in God's heart:
Love to the uttermost
Unending love
Symbol of love
The Cross.

Power from the Cross
To redeem and save,
Power to forgive
And make new.
Power to unite
All men in love,
Power to change
The world.

One at the Cross
Together we kneel,
Gone are the things that divide,
He is our Hope,
He is our Peace
Jesus, the crucified.

Pointing upwards to God,
The Cross
Stretching outwards to men
Lord, draw us all
By the power of your Cross
By your endless self-giving love
To build your Kingdom
In Ireland to-day
And throughout the world.   Amen.

I was witnessing a minor miracle for South Africa. Pretoria Cathedral, right in the heart of the Africaaner capital, was the venue for a "Day of Reconciliation" at which I had been invited to speak. Blacks, whites and coloured from many different denominations spent the day together in worship and prayer and scripture study. Barriers melted away as young and old embraced one another across all the divides that history has created in that land of 'terrible beauty'. Tears of forgiveness flowed. Faith was restored for many who were tempted to despair. Hope returned. Before their eyes they could see a symbol of what that land might be.

Parallels with Ireland

An Irishman is strangely 'at home' in such a scene. Everywhere I spoke about the problems of Ireland and the reconciliation which we were finding in Christ I saw the startling parallels between their situation and ours. The same ingredients are present there – only there are more of them in South Africa. When I spoke of the ignorance and fear, bigotry and prejudice that kept us apart, the bells were ringing for them too.

For 'siege mentality' substitute 'laager mentality'. For 'Prod' and 'Taig' exchange 'Black' and 'White'. And the same catch cries are not far from the surface.

Demonstration Models

The challenge to the Churches in South Africa, as in Ireland, is to translate words into deeds. To provide demonstration models of the healing power of Christ in breaking down the divisions between people and denominations is an urgent task there as here. For those who attempt such experiments there is a heavy cost to be met in rejection, misunderstanding and suffering. The way of the cross is never easy.

One such experiment in South Africa had its origin in the inspiration given by the formation of the Christian Renewal Centre in Rostrevor. Several years ago someone who was burdened by the need to provide a centre of reconciliation in South Africa picked up a leaflet describing the vision behind the Centre for Christian Renewal in Rostrevor. When he read it he said: "If that can happen in Ireland it can happen in South

Africa." After three years a flourishing inter-racial community working for reconciliation is growing. The flowers of hope are pushing out the weeds of hatred and conflict.

Another situation filled us with hope. Billy Johnston from the Shankill Road in Belfast is the Anglican Dean of Zululand. Five years ago he felt very strongly that God was speaking to him and his people about the sin of division in separate worship for different races. Slowly and painfully the parish of Eshowe high up in the hills of Zululand has become a symbol of hope. There we had the great privilege of sharing with many Christians from varied races and backgrounds the joy of healing that comes when 'brothers dwell together in unity'.

Islands of Hope

As I came home from South Africa two scenarios kept moving before my mind's eye. One of bleakness; for, humanly speaking, the outlook is bleak as white pride is met by black pride and the forces of evil seek to create endless havoc. The other scenario I prefer to dwell on; it's a picture of a land of beauty and variety finding a healing through the reconciling, forgiving love of Christ. Join me in praying for that land that more and more islands of hope may spring up amidst an ocean of despair.

I was speaking to a visitor from America the other day. He was here for the first time and he was reflecting on all the tribulation that people are going through in this land. Then he said: "It is as if God was taking you into the forge of His love to test you and make you strong."

His words stirred in me a vivid memory of my childhood. I clearly remember how fascinated I had been by the blacksmith's forge. As a young boy I often went there with my father to have the farm horses re-shod.

Fire, Wind and Water

I recalled that the three elements that are used for the work of God's Spirit in our lives are well illustrated in the forge. Fire, wind and water. When I reflect on the words of my American friend I see what God is doing with many of our lives in this land today.

We are like the metal which the blacksmith takes in his hands. He pumps the bellows and the wind fans the flame. In the red hot coals the metal bends in the hands of the blacksmith. He fashions the metal as he wishes. When it's the way he wants it then he drops it quickly into the water. It's cool and hard and in the shape he has designed. Now it is ready to be used for the purpose he intended.

Instruments in God's Hand

Aren't we like the bare metal? When we allow ourselves to be put into the furnace of God's cleansing love the Master bends and moulds us into the shape He has designed. The wind of God's Spirit fans the flame that is needed to purify us. Immersed in the water of God's life we are made ready for His use – instruments which He can use in the purpose for which He created us.

God loves us too much to leave us as we are.

To Burn Away the Dross

Reflect on these words in the last book of the Old Testament, Malachi 3 vs. 1-3:

> *"Behold, I send my messenger to prepare the way before me, and the Lord whom you seek will suddenly come to his temple; the*

messenger of the covenant in whom you delight, behold, he is coming, says the Lord of hosts. But who can endure the day of his coming, and who can stand when he appears? For he is like a refiner's fire and like fullers' soap; he will sit as a refiner and purifier of silver, and he will purify the sons of Levi and refine them like gold and silver, till they present right offerings to the Lord."

"IF ONLY"

It happened on a farm in one of the great wheat growing areas of the mid-west of the United States. One evening the little girl of the family who owned the farm went missing. Everyone around the farm joined in the search. Darkness fell quickly and the search had to be called off without any trace of the lost child.

Join Hands

At first light all available help was called and the search resumed. After a time of fruitless searching someone made a suggestion. "Let's all join hands", he said "and move together through the wheatfields." They all did that and within half an hour they found the dead body of the little girl. "If only we had joined hands earlier we might have found the girl alive", they said.

Tragic Loss

I often think of that tragic story in relation to what is happening all around us in this land. If we had only joined hands earlier we could have avoided the awful destruction and loss of life that we've experienced here over the past twleve years. Nearly 2,200 people killed and almost 23,000 injured. The sickening statistics tell so little of the misery, tragedy and suffering which we have inflicted on each other.

God's Perfect Love

Patiently Christ waits to heal us of our murdering hate and set us free from the terrible cancer of fear and prejudice which threatens all of us. Only His perfect love can cast out the fear which drives us apart.

I have seen that miracle happen in enough lives to know that it can happen in many more.

From all over Ireland people came in their thousands to Downpatrick on Pentecost Sunday. Four thousand came across the border and as many joined them from different parts of the North.

"Pentecost 81" was the most representative gathering of Christians ever brought together in Ireland. It was such an inspiration to see so many thousands of people proclaim their faith in Jesus Christ as Lord as we sang together:

"We are heirs of the Father
We are joint heirs with the Son
We are children of the Kingdom
We are family, we are one."

A Costly Coming Together

It was painful and costly for many who came. Some were there who had been tragically wounded by the violence. Many were there who had been cruelly bereaved. They had received a supernatural power to forgive. There were men and women there who had been formerly involved in violent activities. Their lives had been radically changed by the power of Christ.

Jesus is the Answer

It was a pilgrimage of HOPE for those who came to Downpatrick on Pentecost Sunday. In the brokenness of our torn world many have lost hope. Many feel despair.

As people came off the buses T.V. crews met them. One woman from Cork was asked why she had come all the way from Cork to Downpatrick for a Service of Repentance and Prayer. She replied: "We are concerned for what's happening in our land". Then with a great smile she said: "But we believe that Jesus is the answer".

Many groups brought banners with them. One that caught my attention had an important message for us all in Ireland today. The banner simply had the words of Jesus: "I MAKE ALL THINGS NEW."

So many people dream of a new Ireland. A NEW IRELAND CAN ONLY BE MADE WITH NEW IRISHMEN. There's only one power that can make us new. That's the power of Christ. Take time today to open your heart to the love of Christ. His power is present now to make you NEW.

93

"A LIGHT TO THE NATIONS"

I never fail to be moved by a visit to Saul near Downpatrick. That is the place where St Patrick first preached the good news of Jesus Christ to the people of Ireland in 432 AD. He preached in a barn which later became a church.

I went to Saul the other day with some friends. It was a blustery morning, one of those days when winter finds it hard to give way to spring. The strong wind tried to blow away the clouds that hung over the hills of Down and rain showers raced over Strangford Lough.

A Better Way
As we prayed there on the hillside the battle between cloud and sunshine seemed to mirror the history of this land since the time of that first preaching of the Gospel. Dark clouds flitting across our history were broken by the sun desperately trying to tell us of a better way and a brighter day.

God of Hope
We prayed in hope, for our God is a God of hope. We can look back with thankfulness on those early days of the young church in this land but we must not look back with nostalgia. Patrick's God is our God still and He wants to do a greater work today than He did then.

A Song of Faith
A few years after his death three thousand Christians, who met every day in Bangor to pray and sing God's praises, gave thanks for Patrick's witness. They prayed and sang in faith. Their inspired words are preserved in the famous "Bangor Antiphonary".

> *"A great light illuminating the world has been kindled, raised on a candlestick, shining over the whole earth, a royal city well fortified and set on a hill, in which there is a great population who belong to God."*

The Dawning of a New Day
When from North and South of this island we come in true repentance and faith to Jesus Christ and turn to Him with all our hearts we shall see a new day dawning for this land. Now a byword among the nations Ireland under God can be again *"a light to the nations"*.

THE CHRISTIAN RENEWAL CENTRE was established in Rostrevor, Co. Down, in August 1974. It is a large house on the shore of Carlingford Lough, near to the border between Northern Ireland and the Irish Republic.

The Centre is staffed by a group of Christians who have been called by God to come together from different traditions in a fellowship of prayer and witness. While remaining members of our own denominations we seek to share our faith in the living Lord Jesus Christ and to pray and work together to encourage the renewal that God by His Holy Spirit is bringing about all over the world.

We believe that Jesus Christ is our way of peace and that through Him we can be truly reconciled to one another.

The Christian Renewal Centre has a three-fold purpose:

1. To be a PLACE OF PRAYER where Christians from all backgrounds may come together in an atmosphere of love and prayer.

2. To be a PLACE OF RENEWAL where people may encounter the living Lord Jesus Christ as the One who baptises in the Holy Spirit and renews His Church to be an effective witness to His power in the world.

3. To be a PLACE OF RECONCILIATION where those who have been separated by ignorance, suspicion and fear may find the reconciliation for which our blessed Lord prays.

The Christian Renewal Centre is a venture in faith and is supported completely by the gifts of God's people. At the outset as we prayed about the Centre, God's Word to us was that "He would put it into the hearts of the right people to give the right amount at the right time."

Acknowledgements

Grateful acknowledgement is made to the Division of Education of the National Council of Churches of Christ in the U.S.A. for quotations from the Revised Standard Version, copyright 1946, 1952 and 1971.

to COLLINS/FONTANA BOOKS for the quotation from *"Something Beautiful for God"* by Malcolm Muggeridge

to MARSHALL, MORGAN AND SCOTT for quote from *"Blow Wind of God"* by Billy Graham

to CONTINENTAL PUBLICATIONS for the quotation *"What God hath promised"* by Annie Johnson Flint

to S.P.C.K. for the quotation from *"The Hard Awakening"* by the Bishop of Iran

to VERITAS PUBLICATIONS for the quotations from *"The Pope in Ireland – Addresses and Homilies"*

to the PUBLISHING DEPARTMENT of the CHURCH OF THE PROVINCE OF SOUTH AFRICA for the quotation re *Maqamusela Kanyile of Zululand.*

to TORCH PUBLISHING CO. LTD for the quotation from *"Henry Francis Lyte"* and *the Story of "Abide with Me"* by Henry James Garland.

to FAIRVIEW PRESS for the quotation from *"Bangor – Light of the World"* by Ian Adamson.